Macroeconomic Strategy for the 1990s

Getting the Long Run Right

Robert A. Levine, Peter J. E. Stan

PREFACE

This report stems from a project on "Public Revenues and Expenditures," the main purpose of which is to provide a thorough-going historical and current analysis of federal, state, and local budgets and finances. This report is meant as a timely contribution to ongoing reexamination of national economic means and ends. By presenting a deliberately contrarian view that questions the importance being given to long-run deficit-busting, it is intended to open up discussion that has been closing down too quickly on the basis of unquestioned assumptions.

The report and the project are supported by RAND, using its own funds. The report is intended to be of interest to the community concerned with national macroeconomic policy.

CONTENTS

FIGURES

TABLES

[In] doing what he did last spring, [Mr. Churchill] was just asking for trouble. . . . Why did he do such a silly thing? Partly, perhaps because he has no instinctive judgement to prevent him from making mistakes; partly because, lacking this instinctive judgement, he was deafened by the clamoring voices of conventional finance; and, most of all, because he was gravely misled by his experts.

—John Maynard Keynes, "The Economic Consequences of
Mr. Churchill" (1925)

The central economic debate in the first half of 1993, couched in terms of short-run economic stimulus versus long-run deficit reduction, may be seriously misleading for U.S. long-run economic strategy itself. The pressures put on the Clinton Administration, from many economists as well as from parts of the Congress, the public, and the press, run the danger of tying the U.S. economy to the wrong goal at the cost of significantly negative effects in both the long run and the short run.

This report makes four key points:

1. **Long run versus short run is a false dichotomy,** since we all live in the short run, and the long run is a series of short runs.

2. **The long-run economic objectives for the United States include the following:**

   • Increasing family standards of living

   • Filling priority needs for public goods

- Maintaining high employment

- Maintaining price stability

- Stabilizing U.S. ownership of the U.S. economy

- Encouraging a distribution of income that the American people find satisfactory.

Rapid and continuing economic growth is central to each objective. We know some things about paths to growth: Many factors may contribute, including education, innovation, and government regulation. Some of the things we think we know are not in accord with the data, however. In particular, the theoretical path that leads from savings to investment to productivity to growth is questionable in its first step. Dollars moved into savings may increase investment, but so may dollars moved out of savings into consumption. And the subsequent steps are equally questionable.

3. **The American economy was not in decline for most of the 1980s.** The 1980s were better than the 1970s, largely because the oil-price problems that dominated the economy of the 1970s disappeared.

4. **Reduction of the federal budget deficit should not be the central objective of long-run economic strategy that it is becoming.** In some ways and at some times, deficit reduction contributes to growth; in some ways and at some times, it detracts from it. Too strong an emphasis on the deficit may depress and distress the U.S. economy through the series of short runs that become the long run. Postponing the filling of urgent public needs can potentially be as imprudent as postponing reduction of the deficit.

A historical parallel to the current emphasis on deficit reduction and other "prudent" long-run "truths" may be found in the British economy of the 1920s, when John Maynard Keynes' essay, "The Economic Consequences of Mr. Churchill," quoted in the epigraph, strongly criticized the then chancellor of the exchequer for listening to his "experts" and tying his nation to the gold standard too early and at too high a level for sterling. The result was a chronic British depression that began a decade before 1933 and exacerbated social divisions that still persist.

THE UNITED STATES' REAL ECONOMIC OBJECTIVES

Accelerating Growth

Although the sources of enhanced living standards are complex, the conventional argument on their increase—one that has had a profound influence on policymaking—goes as follows:

- Real income growth can be sustained only by increasing productivity at a sustainable rate; over the last several decades, the rate of increase in U.S. productivity has decelerated.

- Productivity is increased primarily by increasing capital investment; investment in plant and equipment has been decreasing as a percentage of gross domestic product (GDP).

- Decreased saving by Americans is to blame for decreased investment. The deficit, which is government dissaving in the absence of foreign investment during an era of trade deficits, is the major cause of the decreased saving by the population.

The deficit is thus a major culprit for too-slow increases in standards of living. Public policy to encourage economic growth should therefore focus on deficit reduction.

Each of the steps in this argument is somewhere between dubious and incorrect, particularly in relation to current problems, as the following discussion explains.

Productivity can be measured in a number of ways. Although the measure most used, "output per hour in the business sector," is appropriate for relating inputs to outputs, GDP per member of the population is most relevant to standards of living, because it describes the resources available for use by American consumers. The income-per-person measure bearing directly on living standards increased more rapidly than output per hour in the 1980s, reaching a three-decade peak in 1984. In any case, both measures showed marked improvements in the 1980s as compared with the 1970s, thus throwing into doubt the contention that growth in productivity is on the decline.

Nonetheless, the effect of productivity growth on the standard of living is largely a matter of perception, and it is perceived by many

Americans to have declined. Reasons may include the fact that increases in GDP per person are volatile and have slowed in the last several years; the rapid increase in costs of some goods and services important to the middle class, e.g., housing, higher education, and health care; the declining quality of many public goods; and increasing income inequalities.

Whatever the specific combination, the fingers pointed at long-run declines in the rate of productivity increases as being central to perceived dropoffs in national living standards seem misdirected.

Investment in plant and equipment is only one of a number of factors contributing to increases in productivity, and not the most important one. *Technological change*, defined broadly to include organization of production as well as engineering, contributes twice as much as capital investment as such; and improved worker education is almost as important as new capital equipment, as has been indicated by a number of studies. True, many technological changes are embodied in new capital goods, but policies that emphasize capital goods as such rather than technology miss the central point, and at least some types of public investment (e.g., in education) may enhance the rate of technological change. Moreover, business investment in plant and equipment has been a relatively high proportion of GDP in recent years.

Savings must equal investment as an identity in national income accounting, but that identity is too frequently taken to imply that the rate of saving determines investment, because investment can take place only by spending funds that have been saved rather than used for consumption. The equating mechanism is the interest rate, which by going up when savings are in short supply reduces investment by raising the cost of borrowing investment funds, relative to the potential profit from investing those funds in plant and equipment. The deficit, it is contended, competes for available savings and thus raises the interest rate and reduces investment; deficit reduction will thus increase investment.

In fact, availability of saved funds is only one among a number of factors affecting investment. Another is the market demand for goods to be produced by the capital goods to be invested in, which argues for more, not less, consumption to induce investment. The choice between increased saving and increased consumption depends on specific circumstances at any given time. When the economy is slack, it is difficult to lower interest rates enough to induce investment in the face of pessimistic expectations about the return on the investment. Interest-rate-reduction policies at such times have been likened to "pushing on a string"; policies—including increased deficit-spending—to stimulate increased demand for goods would provide a better prescription.

In the last decade, investment has remained high in spite of the falling rate of personal saving by Americans. As a result, investment has increasingly been financed by foreign countries. If it continues, foreign financing may present real problems for the United States; but it throws into doubt any causal connection between declining U.S. saving rates and investment in the U.S. economy, and thus flagging growth in recent years.

None of this argues that deficit reduction is an inappropriate goal for economic policy. Many economists contend that deficit reduction is desirable: to stabilize foreign ownership of the U.S. economy by limiting foreign investment in the United States; to reduce market distortions caused by the high level of interest payments on the national debt; and, perhaps most important, to lessen the inhibitions the deficit places on public, congressional, and administration willingness to use fiscal policy as a short-run active economic stabilizer and on spending for public needs. But the connection from the deficit, through savings, investment, and productivity, to standards of living, is so tenuous that it should not be allowed to stand in the way of the real goals, as the gold standard did in Britain 70 years ago.

Supplying Needed Public Goods

A second national economic goal is the filling of perceived needs for public goods, whether for investment or consumption. To maintain the long-run focus and stay away from the immediate policy and political controversies surrounding the administration's 1993 proposals, this analysis sets forth an envelope for the costs of public needs that the federal government has been asked to fill. Table S.1 summarizes by major program category either the annual "full-

Table S.1

Annual Federal Full-Funding for Public Needs: The Advocates' View

Need	Funding ($ billions)
Housing and other urban needs. Education, training, and other needs within cities are counted separately.	20
Education, from preschool through higher education. The largest component is for a full preschool program; additional federal aid for kindergarten through high school is the smallest.	50
Training, mostly for a new "apprenticeship" program.	16
Public assistance. The bulk of this would go not for income support as such but for "workfare" and other public jobs.	40
Physical infrastructure. The largest component is for highways, but the total is spread over urban transit, water supply, sewers, etc.	40
International, mostly economic, development assistance to the "third world," at the scope requested by the nations in this category at the Rio environmental conference. Aid to Eastern Europe is substantially less.	50
Space, mostly to put a man on Mars.	11
TOTAL	227

funding" needs estimated by program advocates (e.g., for housing), or, for those programs for which advocates may be motivated to minimize expected costs (e.g., space), the maximum estimates made by skeptics.

Defense is not on the list; it may provide a potential source of funds for other needs. More notably absent, however, is health. *If health costs cannot be contained, then it will be between difficult and impossible to fill other needs, reduce the deficit, or do anything else, as President Clinton himself has recognized.* Estimated costs of national health care reform alone are in the $30–$100 billion range. This analysis, like those questioned here, thus assumes that health-cost problems will be solved—without itself proposing any solutions.

The list of "needs" in Table S.1 is, of course, greatly inflated, providing in each case the highest estimate available. But reducing the figures because they represent the rosy dreams of dedicated advocates, or deciding that much less should be provided to the impoverished of the rest of the world, or dismissing space as a boondoggle, or hoping that the other programs will do away with the welfare population (and that, hence, no increase in public jobs or public assistance payments will be needed) could still ultimately call for around $100 billion a year—less than 2 percent of GDP compared with a deficit currently approaching 5 percent.

That total is lower than is feared by many. In any one year, funds to fill these public needs must compete with funds to reduce the deficit and with funds to provide tax incentives for technological improvement, investment, etc. Public investment must compete with private investment as well.

Maintaining High Employment and Low Inflation

The current short-versus-long-run economic debate ordinarily treats high employment as one of two central short-run goals. The other is maintaining price stability, and high employment and stable prices must be traded off against one another, at least for the short run.

Whether this is true for the long run, or whether policy attempts to achieve long-run high employment will merely increase inflation while failing to improve long-run employment, as is contended by the "rational expectations" school, is a divisive issue in economic theory. Either way, however, the short-run trade-off is clear: Policy-stimulated increases in demand for goods and services, and thus for the jobs that produce those goods and services, will cause firms to some extent to increase production and hiring, and to some extent to raise prices. The mix between the two responses will depend on whether production and employment are slack to begin with and thus easy to increase, or are tight, in which case the major result of stimulus will be increasing prices.

The proper short-run balance between high employment and price stability—and, indeed, whether a choice exists at all in the light of the arguments made by the rational expectations theorists—is a function of conditions at the time. Whatever the chosen mix, however, we should remember that the long run is a series of short runs: If stimulus can produce short-run growth over a series of periods, the result may be higher standards of living over the long run, especially if expectations are less than fully rational.

Such a tilt toward long-run growth also implies some degree of long-run inflation, however. Through the 1960s, price increases of 2–3 percent per year were generally considered acceptable—and even desirable—in the United States; less would have required downward price flexibility that would have been difficult and painful to achieve with the institutions of a modern economy and society.

In the years after the first oil shock in 1973, however, average annual inflation rose to almost 10 percent, largely because of that shock and subsequent ones; it was almost 15 percent for 1980. Such inflation had traumatic effects on the political economy. It led some American economists to fear the kind of hyper-inflation that had occurred elsewhere, notably in Germany after both world wars (forgetting that Germany's and other cases of hyper-inflation stemmed from economies that were very different from the U.S. economy of the 1970s). One result is that, even now, a dozen years later, when the evidence is clear that the decade of the 1970s was a special case because of the oil shocks, some economists, including the leadership of the Federal Reserve System, adhere to a zero- or near-zero-inflation goal in spite of the negative short- and long-run effects on growth and employment. And politically, the "stagflation" of the 1970s—the condition in which all available policy choices combined politically unacceptable levels of unemployment and inflation—contributed to the fall of the governments of all major Western industrial states in the short period between 1979 and 1982.

In the United States, the new administration must now choose a short-run combination of employment levels and rates of inflation. This analysis does not examine that choice, but it does contend that the mix should be weighted toward short-run considerations, and the deficit should be only one among many factors. The menu of possibilities in 1993 is far more flexible and acceptable than those in 1979 and 1980, given the lack of double-digit inflation and unemployment, and current choices should be much easier to make.

POLICY CONCLUSIONS

The strongest conclusion is the negative one:

> Reduction of the budget deficit should not be the central objective of long-run strategy. Too strong an emphasis on the deficit may depress and distress the U.S. economy over a very long run.

This conclusion has a number of implications for current economic policy:

- Reduced emphasis on deficit reduction implies greater emphasis on short-run considerations than would otherwise be the case, but specific current policy should be evaluated on the basis of specific current data.

- Omitting concerns about income and wealth distribution, increasing standards of living continue to depend on increasing productivity. Since increasing productivity depends more on technological advance than on investment as such, policy incentives should focus on such advance, and on education and training as well as private investment.

- Increasing private investment, and expenditures on technology as well, may depend in any given situation on consumer demand at least as much as on increased personal saving.

- Both public and private investment can increase productivity, and choices between the two should be based on specifics.

- Public amenities (e.g., parks) also have a place in the competition. The total of public needs for investment and amenities, even as represented by their advocates, is high but not so overwhelming as to paralyze decisions until the deficit is "solved."

- The deficit cannot and should not be ignored. Plausible goals for deficit reduction should be based on the need to reduce the proportion of GDP going to interest payments on the national debt and should be timed with due regard for the other, more basic, long-run goals.

But to avoid economic consequences in the 1990s that resemble the economic consequences of Mr. Churchill in the 1920s, the administration and the Congress should resist the pressures to dwell almost exclusively on deficit reduction; they should base economic strategy on the real economic goals of the United States.

ACKNOWLEDGMENTS

The authors wish to thank their RAND colleagues Stephen Drezner, James Hosek, and Stanley Panis and RAND trustee and consultant Charles Zwick for very useful comments on earlier drafts of this report. Not all of them will agree with the conclusions.

Chapter One

WHAT ARE THE OBJECTIVES?

[In] doing what he did last spring, [Mr. Churchill] was just asking for trouble. . . . Why did he do such a silly thing? Partly, perhaps because he has no instinctive judgement to prevent him from making mistakes; partly because, lacking this instinctive judgement, he was deafened by the clamoring voices of conventional finance; and, most of all, because he was gravely misled by his experts.

—John Maynard Keynes
"The Economic Consequences of Mr. Churchill" (1925)

[One major] reason to cut the budget deficit is to speed up the growth of American productivity and living standards, which for the past two decades has been very sluggish. . . . Like a private family, the country can raise its future living standards if it summons the will to forego some private and public consumption today in order to invest the savings in productive income-producing assets.[1]

—Charles L. Schultze (1993)

THE LONG RUN AND THE SHORT RUN

This report about U.S. macroeconomic policy was written in 1993, but it concerns only indirectly the most widely discussed issue of the first half of that year: economic stimulus versus deficit reduction. The use of the word *strategy* in the title implies a focus on long-run policy—over the next four or eight years. To many economists, ex-

---

[1]Charles L. Schultze, "Why We Can't Put Off Reducing the Deficit," *USA Today*, February 16, 1993, p. 11A.

emplified by the Brookings Institution's Charles Schultze, who had been President Johnson's budget director and chairman of President Carter's Council of Economic Advisers, and to large segments of the Congress, the public, and the press, the central aim of such long-run macroeconomic policy must be deficit reduction. The contention here, however, is that *it is misleading to couch the central issue as stimulus versus deficit reduction, with stimulus as a short-run objective and deficit reduction as a long-run strategy. Such a false contraposition is likely to set long-run strategy in the wrong direction.*

Keynes' essay on Churchill's tenure as chancellor of the exchequer is a reminder of the fact that, although we economic "experts" like to espouse the stern discipline of the long run as against the feel-good political remedies of the short run, unexamined and dubious goals for the long run can lead to distress both short and long. In the 1920s, Keynes argued that the "silly thing" done by Churchill, following his experts, was to deflate the British economy by returning to the gold standard, too early and at too high a level for sterling. Keynes was right. The results turned out to be a decade of British unemployment above 10 percent *before* the Depression; the General Strike of 1926; and the perpetuation of class hatreds that remain a major factor in Britain even now. The football hooligans are Churchill's grandchildren.

The policy implications of this history complement those of the better-known Keynes statement, not ordinarily quoted in full:

> But this *long run* is a misleading guide to current affairs. *In the long run* we are all dead. Economists set themselves too easy, too useless a task if in tempestuous seasons they can only tell us that when the storm is long past the ocean is flat again.[2]

For the United States in 1993, the analogy to the long-run gold-standard grail of Churchill and his experts is the absolute priority given by some to closing the deficit. If, as argued here, deficit-closing is no more than a partial and imperfect proxy for more basic long-run objectives—indeed, more a result of achieving those objectives than a

---

[2]John Maynard Keynes, *A Tract on Monetary Reform,* Macmillan, London, 1929, p. 80. [Italics in original.]

means of achieving them—then the entire set of macroeconomic policy alternatives needs to be recast.

WHAT ARE THE REAL OBJECTIVES?

The deficit is a construct that *directly* affects the economic well-being of nobody: If closing it helps achieve real objectives for the nation and the American people, then it should be closed; under some circumstances, perhaps, it should be increased. The same agnosticism should be applied to another frequently claimed goal, increased national savings; it should be applied to increased investment; it should be applied even to increased productivity. Each of these interrelated aims is important only insofar as it contributes to more fundamental economic goals. In fact, most of them do contribute, but how they do so is not a simple matter.

A basic list of long-run economic goals might include the following:

- *Increasing standards of living for families and individuals.* Such an increase ordinarily requires continuing economic growth that is more rapid than population growth. Although increasing standards can be achieved temporarily by borrowing from abroad, as in the 1980s, or by dipping into savings, the eventual payback is likely to require decreasing standards.

- *Filling needs for those public goods defined by a majority.* Some standard public goods (e.g., highways) contribute to productivity and living standards. Others (e.g, national parks) may be desirable in themselves. This report does not emphasize that distinction.

- *Maintaining high levels of employment.* It might be economically possible to maintain high average living standards in spite of relatively low aggregate employment, by rapid growth in some sectors underpinned by a generous system of unemployment benefits and subsidies for other sectors. Such a phenomenon seems to have happened, at least for a while, in Thatcherite Britain, but it is not likely to be acceptable in the United States.

- *Maintaining stability of prices paid by consumers.* As will be discussed, attempts to achieve zero inflation may do severe harm to other goals, including rapid growth and high employment, but substantial price stability is both instrumental to other goals and in itself a consensus goal.

- *Stabilizing American ownership of the American economy.* Although increasing international economic interdependence is inevitable and probably desirable, and border-crossing investment is a necessary part of that interdependence, most Americans probably would most prefer the U.S. economy to be controlled by Americans.

- *Moving toward some desired pattern in the distribution of economic rewards.* This is deliberately kept vague. In principle, most Americans would favor providing a serious safety net at the bottom of the income distribution. It is not a central topic of this report but is mentioned because many economists, finding distribution difficult to handle, set it aside as a policy concern, and that is not intended here.

The focus of the report is on the first four goals—increasing living standards (Chapter Two), filling needs for public goods (Chapter Three), maintaining high employment, and maintaining price stability; because high employment and price stability are frequently considered in terms of trade-offs between the two, they are discussed together (in Chapter Four). The other two goals, stabilizing American ownership of the American economy and affecting the distribution of economic rewards, are outside the central macroeconomic focus here; they are mentioned mainly as they relate to the four primary goals.

Chapter Two

INCREASING STANDARDS OF LIVING

Increasing standards of living is the most discussed and the most basic of the goals: that, in general, next year will be better economically than this; and that our children will be better off than we were. It obviously does not apply to every year, every family, or every individual. But if living standards increase on the average for the United States as a whole, they will increase for most of the people most of the time. And, very important for a stable society, such general increases mean that changes in *relative* standards will take place mostly by differential relative rates of positive growth, rather than every increase for someone having to be matched by a decrease for someone else.

The conventional argument on increasing living standards as a current policy issue is that, unless we are to borrow from abroad, which is obviously unsustainable although we did it throughout the 1980s, or dip into savings, also unsustainable, such increases ordinarily take the following three steps:

- Standards may be increased only by increasing productivity, i.e., goods and service produced per unit of input. Over the last one, two, and three decades, we have increased productivity at a decreasing rate.

- Productivity is increased primarily by increasing investment in capital goods. Investment has been decreasing in the U.S. economy.

- Because, as an accounting identity in a simple model based on national income accounts, *investment* (defined as goods produced but not used for personal consumption) must be equal to *savings* (income received and not spent on personal consumption), decreased saving by Americans is to blame for decreased investment and therefore for deceleration of productivity increases. The deficit, which is government dissaving in the absence of a trade surplus, is the major cause of the decreased saving by the population.

This is an admittedly oversimplified version of the argument, but the conclusion—that the deficit is thus the primary culprit for too-slow increases in productivity, growth, and standards of living—is at the core of much of the current discourse on economic policy.

Each of the three steps in the above argument is somewhere between dubious and incorrect. Productivity increases have dropped sharply in the last several years. But they may be cyclical; the 1980s were substantially better than the 1970s. Investment has been a relatively minor contributor to increased productivity, and in recent years investment has, at worst, held steady. Saving is only one of many influences on investment, but, in any case, decreased savings have had little visible effect on investment.

Rather, a quite different and more logical argument does connect government spending and deficits with deceleration in the growth of living standards. It has to do with public-versus-private competition for resources. But the proper balance between the two, for maximum growth, cannot be determined by logic alone. These issues are taken up in the concluding chapter (Chapter Five). The remainder of this chapter examines the flawed three-step chain of conventional reasoning about standards of living.

PRODUCTIVITY

The argument that for living standards to increase, goods and services produced per unit of input (i.e., *productivity* as ordinarily defined) must increase, is based on sound logic, but it lacks a step. Putting in that step and examining the data over the past three decades throw into question any simple attribution of reduced living standards to reduced productivity in that period.

The contention in this section differs from that put forward by a number of recent papers, which have contended that U.S. productivity data are in themselves flawed, largely because they do not take adequate account of changes in the composition of production (e.g., the mix between goods and services) or of the quality of goods produced.[1] Those analyses reinforce (or are reinforced by) the arguments here, which suggest additional doubts even on the basis of conventional data on productivity and gross domestic product (GDP).

What is suggested here is

- First, that although *labor productivity*, defined by the U.S. Department of Labor as "output per hour in the business sector," is the appropriate measure for many purposes—e.g., relating inputs to outputs and examining international competitiveness—standards of living have directly to do not with productive *inputs* in that sector or the economy as a whole but with *receipt* of income by all those who benefit from that income. Thus, GDP *per member of the population* must be examined, too.

- Second, that when both measures are examined over time, it is not obvious that the growth of American productivity has slowed to a historically disturbing rate. This statement is particularly true of the GDP-per-person measure, in which current short-run changes may be skewing perceptions about the long run.

Table 2.1 shows the two productivity measures averaged over various time periods, the conventional way of presenting such data. The first three lines are the most conventional, using averages by decade (although, unconventionally, in order to take advantage of the latest data, the decades are slipped by one year). They show that by the input–output measure, the conventional belief is borne out: Productivity increases have slipped badly. Using the GDP-per-person measure, however, the 1980s, while still below the end-of-the-postwar decade of the 1960s, improved quite a bit over that of the

---

[1] See, for example, James K. Galbraith, "A New Picture of the American Economy," *The American Prospect*, Fall 1991; and Michael Darby, "Causes of Declining Growth," Paper presented to the Symposium on Policies for Long-Run Economic Growth, Federal Reserve Bank of Kansas City, 1992.

Table 2.1

Two Concepts of U.S. Productivity Change: Various Periods

		Average Annual Percentage Change	
Time Period Averaged Over		Product per Hour, Business Sector	Real GDP per Population Member, 14 and older
1.	1962–1971	2.8	2.2
2.	1972–1981	1.0	0.7
3.	1982–1991	1.0	1.2
4.	1962–1973	2.8	2.2
5.	1974–1980	0.5	0.2
6.	1981–1991	1.1	1.2
7.	1981–1988	1.4	1.6

SOURCE: *Economic Report of the President, 1992*, U.S. Government Printing Office, Washington, D.C., February 1992, Tables B-2, B-30, and B-45.

1970s. (And, contrary to conventional wisdom, U.S. productivity growth in the 1980s was more rapid than that of West Germany or the European Community as a whole, although still slower than Japan's.)

Over what period the measure is taken also makes a big difference. Substituting for arbitrary decades, distinguishable economic periods—from the 1960s through the first oil shock consequent upon the Yom Kippur War in late 1973—the fourth line shows that productivity growth remained rapid by both measures. From the first oil shock to the end of the second consequent upon the 1980 release of the American hostages in Teheran, it was very low (line 5): The rewards went to the overseas oil cartel, not to American labor. But when oil prices began to drop after 1980 (line 6), U.S. productivity began to recover. Indeed, the average annual rates of change between two peaks in productivity growth, 1981 and 1988, are even higher, as shown by the last line; the standard-of-living rate even approaches that of the palmy 1960s.

None of these data prove much, except that averages over periods do not capture the appropriate phenomena. By looking at each year of change, however, Figure 2.1 throws more light on the issue. The line showing production per hour (OP/hr) indicates that this traditional measure has in fact been declining: Successive peak growth rates, for example, drop from 4.3 percent in 1964 to 3.6 percent in 1971 to 3.0 percent in 1976 to 2.3 percent in 1984. The GDP-per-person measure, however, fell less over the three decades but was more volatile over short periods. It actually reached its highest annual level over the entire period in 1984—4.9 percent as compared with the 4.6 of 1966. GDP per person dropped faster than output per hour in the years when it did fall, however.

Indeed, given the fact that standard of living is to a great extent a matter of perceptions, and perceptions fade over time, perhaps the major phenomenon underlying the belief in a long-run decline is the sharp year-by-year drop from the 1984 peak to 1991, the latest year for which data are available. Seven years is a long enough time to set perceptions. The real question, however, is, When GDP per person does begin to rise again, will its next peak be as high as that of the 1980s, or will it follow the long-run decline of production per hour (or might production per hour itself begin to turn up)?

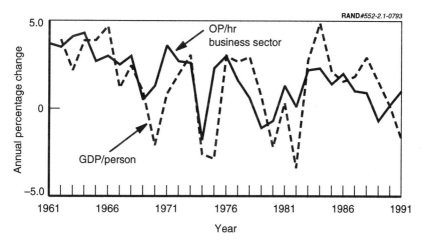

SOURCE: *Economic Report of the President, 1992,* U.S. Government Printing Office, Washington, D.C., February 1992, Tables B-2, B-30, and B-45.

OP = output

Figure 2.1—Two Concepts of U.S. Productivity Change

In any case, in addition to the recent fall of GDP per person, other perceptions that may influence the general belief that living standards have been declining include the following facts:

- The costs relative to income of some goods and services central to middle-class perceptions have gone up sharply in recent years. Examples include housing, higher education, and health care.

- The quality of some public goods forming an important part of standards of living (e.g., primary and secondary education) has declined, even though expenditures for students have, on the average, gone up during this period.

- The productivity figures illustrated in Figure 2.1 are national averages. Redistribution of income toward the better-off in the 1980s[2] may have hurt the standards of living of many families and individuals.

Whatever the combination of reasons, however, the perceived slowdown in growth of national living standards over a period of time is at best due only in part to a slowdown of productivity growth.

INVESTMENT

Withal, the faster that productivity by any measure increases, the faster standards of living will increase. How to increase productivity? The conventional prescription is to increase capital investment: the more capital in use by each worker, the higher will be at least labor productivity, and perhaps the productivity of all factors of production including capital itself. Again, this statement is correct but incomplete:

- Capital is a surprisingly minor contributor to productivity growth.

---

[2]See Lynn A. Karoly, "The Widening Income and Wage Gap Between Rich and Poor: Trends, Causes, and Policy Options," in James B. Steinberg, David W. Lyon, and Mary E. Vaiana, eds., *Urban America: Policy Choices for Los Angeles and the Nation*, MR-100-RC, RAND, Santa Monica, Calif., 1992.

- Capital investment in the United States has not been going down; it has been holding quite steady.

Table 2.2 shows estimates of the contributions to growth in the productivity of labor attributable to several sets of contributors.[3]   By these estimates, increases in capital stock (i.e., investment) provide only one-quarter of the positive contributions to productivity, little more than increases in worker productivity attributable to better education and consequent greater skills of the workers themselves. "Technological advance" on the other hand, defined here to include both the Table 2.2 categories of "Advances in knowledge" applied to production and improved productive organization as embodied in

Table 2.2

Contributions to Increasing Labor Productivity, 1929–1982

Contributor	Percentage Contributed (%)
Capital	25
Advances in knowledge	36
Improved resource allocation	10
Education per worker	18
Economies of scale	12
TOTAL	100

SOURCE: Computed from Edward F. Denison, *Trends in American Economic Growth, 1929–1982*, Brookings Institution, Washington, D.C., 1985, p. 30 (table).

---

[3]The estimates are computed from the table on p.30 of Edward F. Denison, *Trends in American Economic Growth, 1929–1982*, Brookings Institution, Washington, D.C., 1985. Denison is the acknowledged expert in this field. The computations here are based on column 5 of his table, providing estimates for contributions to growth of actual national income (rather than potential national income) in the whole economy (rather than nonresidential business) for total population (rather than per person employed). Denison's table shows contributions to aggregate economic growth, including the contribution made by increases in numbers of workers (32 percent). To convert them to contributions to the productivity *of labor*, the estimates here remove the contribution attributed to worker numbers.   They also remove negative "contributions" he assigns to a miscellany of factors.

"Improved resource allocation," accounts for much of the lion's share—almost half.

The proportions accord with most modern empirical theory: Technological change and improved education and skills, rather than simple increase of capital stock, are responsible for most growth. *To be sure, most of the technological change must be embodied in new capital,* but the important contributor is the type of capital, not its quantity. The policy implications will be discussed in the last chapter of this report. But for now, the crucial role of technological advance represents another break in the conventional chain leading from standard of living through productivity and investment to savings.

That is not the entire argument about investment, however. Capital investment does contribute to productivity growth, even if only 25 percent. But investment has not contributed to any decline in American productivity because investment has not declined. Figure 2.2 shows business spending on new plant and equipment as a

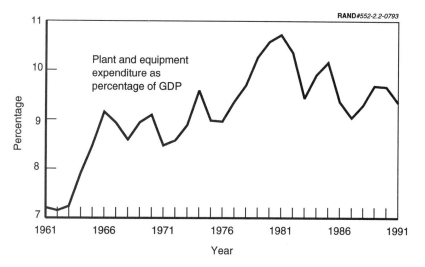

SOURCE: *Economic Report of the President, 1992,* Tables B-1 and B-52.

Figure 2.2—Business Spending on New Plant and Equipment as Percentage of GDP

percentage of gross domestic product. Although such investment in recent years has been lower than the peak achieved in the late 1970s and the early 1980s, it has been roughly equal to or higher than it was through most of the 1960s and 1970s. Current shortfalls in productivity, if any, do not stem from historically low investment— another weak link in the conventional chain.

SAVINGS

The third link is the contention that investment is low because savings are low. The theoretical argument is based on the definitions (approximately) of investment in national income accounting as private product minus consumption, and savings as private income minus income spent on consumption. Investment must thus equal savings, by definition.[4] If savings are low or declining, investment must be low or declining. And private savings are low because the deficit takes these savings and puts them into public spending rather than making them available for private investment. *Ergo,* the deficit is the culprit.

The argument has two flaws: the purely empirical one, that the relationship between domestic savings and investment is not demonstrable in three decades of data; and the theoretical one, that savings are only one of a number of important influences on investment.

Figure 2.3 repeats the line of Figure 2.2 for business spending on plant and equipment as a percentage of GDP, and adds a line showing savings as a percentage of personal income over the same period (1961 = 100 for both lines). A discerning eye may be able to detect lagged patterns, trends, or whatever in the figure; or a complex econometric model may dig them out. That such patterns exist is likely, but the low correlation and lack of any easily visible

---

[4]This definition is deliberately simplified. The full equation shows that private investment plus government spending on goods and services equal savings plus the balance-of-payments deficit. Omitting government spending makes the argument here that decreased savings have not decreased private investment, *a fortiori;* increased government spending on goods and services in the 1980s should have pushed private investment down further. Putting the balance-of-payments deficit back in the picture will be used below to help explain the conundrum.

relationship make the key point: that saving is only one of many influences on investment.

Other influences, each of which can lay at least as good an *a priori* claim as savings to being a determinant of investment include the following:

*   *Market demand.* Seeing a market out there for the goods made by the capital goods to be invested in is generally considered a major incentive for investment. Indeed, "accelerator" theories suggest that an increase in demand will have a magnified effect because it will call for a proportional increase in capital *stock*, with investment, the first derivative of capital stock, rising much more rapidly than, rather than in proportion to, the increase in demand. Be that as it may, it is important to note that the demand "pull" on investment is a direct rival to the savings "push," because any given spendable dollar may go into consumption or other direct spending on goods and services, or may be held back in savings, but cannot go into both. One recent

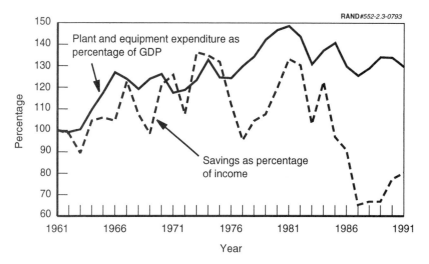

SOURCE: *Economic Report of the President, 1992*, Tables B-1, B-24, and B-52.

Figure 2.3—New Plant and Equipment as Percentage of GDP and Savings as Percentage of National Income

paper suggested on different pages that "economic growth may not be as robust as during the 1980s because . . . consumer demand growth is likely to remain sluggish," and that growth policy should "encourage Net National Saving . . . by reducing or even reversing tax incentives for debt and consumption over saving and investment."[5] These two statements are incompatible, and *the choice in any given situation between demand-pull and savings-push as an inducement to investment is a crucial one for economic policy.*

- *After-tax returns.* The higher the expected rate of return on an investment, the more likely that investment becomes. Increasing expected rates by cutting the portion to be taken in taxes can be a powerful incentive to increased investment; that was a truth hidden inside the legitimate version of supply-side economics, before it was taken to extremes. What taxes at what rates on what investments is a difficult and detailed question, however, particularly since the earlier argument implies that it is more important to encourage technological advance than capital investment as such.

- *Innovation.* Joseph Schumpeter attributed most growth to the process of innovation, by which entrepreneurs brought into economic being—from invention through production to marketing—new inventions, products, processes, and modes of organization.[6] The great waves of growth-inducing innovation included the steam engine/industrial revolution, the railroad revolution of the last half of the nineteenth century, the automobile and airplane, the chemical revolution,[7] and, since Schumpeter, the electronic and now perhaps the biotechnical revolutions. How government policy may encourage innovative growth is a difficult question; Schumpeter thought that government policy mostly inhibited it.

---

[5]Michael Calabrese and Maureen Steinbrunner, "Discussion Paper on Tax Revenue and Restructuring: Problems, Principles, and Prototypes," Paper prepared for the Advisory Group of the Center for National Policy, Washington, D.C., November 19, 1992, pp. 7 and 9.

[6]Joseph A. Schumpeter, *The Theory of Economic Development*, Harvard University Press, Cambridge, Mass., 1936.

[7]Joseph A. Schumpeter, *Business Cycles* (two volumes), McGraw-Hill, New York, 1939.

This argument does not imply, however, that savings are irrelevant to investment. Quite the contrary, investment in some sense must be paid for by savings, even if the investment has been induced by consumption increases that have reduced savings.

Another means of financing investment in the United States, however, is by foreign savings; here is where the balance of payments deficit comes back into the equation. When the balance is negative, the surplus of imports over exports is financed by foreign funds flowing into U.S. capital markets. In recent years, this flow has been rapid. From 1982, when data were first gathered, to 1990, foreign ownership of private assets in the United States increased from $524.4 billion to $1,793.2 billion, an average of $158.6 billion per year in new foreign investment.[8] U.S. personal savings averaged $180.2 billion per year over the same period.[9] Although the two figures are not precisely comparable, nor do they provide the only sources of investment funds for the United States (corporate savings in particular must be added in), they do show—dramatically—that new investment in the United States has become almost as dependent on foreign savings as on the personal savings of Americans. Indeed, comparing foreign ownership of U.S. private assets to total U.S. private wealth, from 1982 to 1990, foreign ownership *doubled* in proportion, from 5.2 percent to 10.5 percent.[10]

Underinvestment in the United States because of undersaving in the United States has not been a problem, even in the 1980s. The fact that U.S. investment has increasingly been financed from abroad, and that non-Americans have thus come to own an increasing share of American private assets, however, could become a real problem in the future, if the flow is suddenly cut off or if the rights of ownership are aggressively asserted. It, not our failure to grow because the profligacy of our consumption reduces investment in our economy, may be an issue for the 1990s.

---

[8]Computed from *Economic Report of the President, 1992*, Table B-99.

[9]Ibid., Table B-24.

[10]Ibid., Tables B-99 and B-109. These figures are also not strictly comparable, but they indicate orders of magnitude.

THE BROKEN CHAIN: POLICY IMPLICATIONS

To summarize the argument thus far:

- Whatever has been happening to U.S. standards of living is not directly due to reduced U.S. productivity.
- Whatever has been happening to productivity is not directly due to reduced investment.
- Whatever has been happening to investment is not directly due to reduced savings or the increased deficit.

Nonetheless, it may still be desirable to reduce the deficit, for three reasons: to stabilize foreign ownership of U.S. private and public assets, at levels low enough to avoid questions of the political effects of possible attempts to exert ownership control; to reduce market distortions caused by the high level of interest payments on the national debt; and to reduce the inhibitions the deficit itself exerts on public, congressional, and administration willingness to use fiscal policy as an active economic stabilizer and to spend for public needs. The last reason is discussed in the next chapter.

Breaking the chain of theories from high deficits to low standards of living does mean, however, that reduction of the U.S. federal deficit in the 1990s, like Britain's return to the gold standard in the 1920s, need not be so urgent a long-run objective as to either wipe out all other long-run objectives or to force Americans to tolerate a series of short-run austerities that could add up to long-run misery. At least in the Keynesian version, when the economy is hot enough to need cooling down, perhaps even when it is warm enough to tolerate some constraint, deficit reduction should become a priority. But the paradox is that then it will not have to be a priority because a strong economy and rapid growth will show themselves to be the best means of deficit reduction in any case. In the meantime, however, when economic stimulus may be needed, deficit reduction should not become the prime short-run goal. As noted at the beginning, this report takes no stand on which condition now prevails but merely notes that deficit reduction should not be at the top of the list either way.

Chapter Three

FILLING PUBLIC NEEDS AND PUBLIC COSTS

The deficit to be reduced, when it is reduced, now ranges around $300 billion per year. Other long-run needs, rivals to deficit reduction for tax dollars, come to less, maybe even a lot less. To maintain the long-run focus and stay away from the immediate policy and political controversies of 1993, this analysis provides instead an envelope for the costs of public needs that the federal government has been asked to fill. Table 3.1 summarizes, by major program category, either the annual "full-funding" needs estimated by program advocates (e.g., for housing) or, for those programs for which advocates may be motivated to minimize expected costs (e.g., space), the maximum estimates made by skeptics. The Appendix provides sources and detail for these estimates.

Notably absent from the list is health. If health costs cannot be reduced, then it will be between difficult and impossible to fill other needs, reduce the deficit, or do anything else. For example, estimated costs of national health care reform alone are in the $30–$100 billion range. This analysis, like those questioned here, thus assumes that health-cost problems will be solved—without itself proposing any solutions. Nor is defense on the list; it may provide a potential source of funds for other needs.

The list of "needs" is, of course, greatly inflated. But reducing the figures because they represent the rosy dreams of dedicated advocates, or deciding that much less should be provided to the impoverished of the rest of the world, or dismissing space as a boondoggle, or hoping that the other programs will do away with the welfare popu-

Table 3.1

Annual Federal Full-Funding for Public Needs: The Advocates' View

Need	Funding ($ billions)
Housing and other urban needs. Education, training, and other needs within cities are counted separately.	20
Education, from preschool through higher education. The largest component is for a full preschool program; additional federal aid for kindergarten through high school is the smallest.	50
Training, mostly for a new "apprenticeship" program.	16
Public assistance. The bulk of this would go not for income support as such but for "workfare" and other public jobs.	40
Physical infrastructure. The largest component is for highways, but the total is spread over urban transit, water supply, sewers, etc.	40
International, mostly economic, development assistance to the "third world," at the scope requested by the nations in this category at the Rio environmental conference. Aid to Eastern Europe is substantially less.	50
Space, mostly to put a man on Mars.	11
TOTAL	227

SOURCES: The Appendix provides more detail on the programs within each category. The sources were primarily public reports on various estimates, as printed in newspapers, magazines, and journals. In addition, the Congressional Budget Office (CBO) provided help in interpreting some of them, particularly in the "Physical infrastructure" category.

lation—and that, hence, no increase in public jobs or public assistance payments will be needed—might still leave the total that could ultimately be called for around $100 billion per year.

That total is much lower than the deficit itself and probably much lower than is feared by many. In any one year, funds to fill these public needs must compete with funds to reduce the deficit, and funds to provide tax incentives for technological improvement, investment, etc. The nature of that competition—both between public and private productivity-increasing investment, and between investment and desired public amenities—will be treated in the concluding chapter of this analysis. What is important here, however, is that the needs are not so overwhelming as to be set aside while the deficit and other matters are disposed of. Filling priority needs should be an important competitor for funds from the beginning.

Chapter Four

MAINTAINING HIGH EMPLOYMENT
AND LOW INFLATION

Issues of employment and inflation form part of the short-run discussion about stimulus versus deficit reduction. How much deficit reduction might increase national saving depends somewhat on whether the deficit is reduced by cutting government spending or increasing taxes. As a practical matter, any substantial program of deficit reduction will involve both, and since the magnitude of economic effects associated with each will differ,[1] the outcome will depend on the particular mix. The Congressional Budget Office has estimated that a mixed approach to eliminating the federal deficit by 1998 could increase national saving by around 5 percent of GDP in 2003. They state that the increase in saving could, in turn, add more than 5 percent to the sustainable level of consumption after that time.[2]

Employment and inflation are also important strategic issues, however; high employment and stable prices are in themselves central

---

[1] In particular, a spending reduction is likely to reduce GDP by a greater amount than a tax increase of equal size, because a tax increase will reduce saving in some measure, as well as consumption. In addition, however, Barro's "Ricardian Equivalence" result suggests that, at a constant level of government expenditure, any increase in taxes that reduces the deficit may have an added expansionary effect because, by lowering the deficit, it induces expectations of future tax cuts and thus increases consumption. (See, e.g., Robert J. Barro, "The Ricardian Approach to Budget Deficits," *Journal of Economic Perspectives,* Vol. III, 1989, pp. 37–54.) The theoretical underpinnings of Barro's argument, however, have been questioned by B. Douglas Bernheim and Kyle Bagwell ("Is Everything Neutral?" *Journal of Political Economy,* Vol. LI, 1989, p. 310).

[2] Congressional Budget Office, *The Economic and Budget Outlook: Fiscal Years 1994–1998,* Washington, D.C., January 1993, pp. 74–75.

long-run goals, and they interact with the other major goals. What the employment and price goals themselves should be, separately and as a combination, is largely a question of political choice. Indeed, in most industrial economies, it is the central choice, with success or failure measurable in terms of political outcomes.

Economically, however, high employment and low inflation must ordinarily be traded off against one another, at least for the short run. At any given time, the most effective way for public policy to increase employment is to increase the demand for goods and the labor producing those goods, by increasing government spending or by inducing increases in private spending via reductions in taxes or interest rates. The dilemma is that increasing demand will increase not only production and employment; part of the response by suppliers of goods and labor will be to raise prices and wages. If employment is low to begin with, it can be hoped that most of the effect of the demand increase will be an increase in jobs; but if demand goes up when employment is already high, price and wage raises will be the primary result. And, conversely, attempts to lower prices or slow inflation by reducing demand will also reduce production and employment, with the division between price and production effects depending on the going-in state of employment.

The trade-off phenomenon is a conceptually simple one, which, because of its elegant analytical demonstration in 1958 by A.W. Phillips, is frequently known as the "Phillips Curve."[3] In the 1970s, a number of economists questioned at least the long-run validity of the Phillips Curve, proposing instead the "rational expectations" theory: that demand-stimulus policies to increase employment would be vitiated by price- and wage-setters' expectations that such policies would be inflationary, and their consequent attempts to get ahead of the game by raising prices right away rather than increasing production and employment.[4] The critics themselves were criticized,[5] but the point

---

[3]A. W. Phillips, "The Relation Between Unemployment and the Rate of Change of Money Wage Rates in the United Kingdom, 1861–1957," *Economica*, November 1958.

[4]See, in particular, Thomas Sargent and Neil Wallace, "Rational Expectations, the Optimal Money Instrument, and the Optimal Money Supply Rule," *Journal of Political Economy*, Vol. XXXVII, 1975.

[5]For example, James Tobin, "Current Controversies in Macroeconomics," *Harvard Graduate Society Newsletter*, Fall 1990.

here is not to enter this doctrinal thicket but rather to suggest that even if rational expectations theory is correct, it need not automatically provide answers for current policy.

Perhaps rational expectations do provide a correct view of a long-run equilibrium: At the end of some period of time, a demand stimulus to the economy will have dissipated, with production and employment being the same as they would have been without it, but prices higher than they would have been. For a while in the 1970s, it seemed that the same might be true in the short run; inflationary expectations stemming from demand stimulus would immediately be subsumed into prices, with little production–employment effect. That may have been a phenomenon of the oil-shocked times, however, as discussed below.[6] It now seems likely that, even if rational expectations were to provide an accurate description of long-run equilibrium, the trade-off doctrine could have substantial validity at least for the short run: Demand stimulus, when the economy is in recession or slow growth, will increase production and employment, and accelerate growth. (Whether a stimulus policy can be timed to be effective before the situation has changed and reverse policies are called for is another question, which is avoided here by staying away from current stimulus issues.)

More fundamentally, however, the long run is a series of short runs. And if short-run stimulus policy can promote more rapid growth than would otherwise have been the case over this series, and if expectations are less-than-fully rational, these conditions will assist in achieving the basic goals of higher standards of living and higher employment. On the other hand, however, few will be worse off if long-run inflation becomes more rapid than it might have been. In 1991, consumer prices in the United States were roughly *4-1/2 times as high* as in 1961. Aside from some nostalgia about prices of bread, postage stamps, and subway rides, nobody much cared; and little nostalgia is expressed for 1961 incomes. Had inflation been steady at the 5-percent annual rate that would have compounded to 450 per-

---

[6]Albert Ando, Flint Brayton, and Arthur Kennickell, "Reappraisal of the Phillips Curve and Direct Effects of Money Supply on Inflation" (in Lawrence R. Klein, ed., *Comparative Performance of U.S. Econometric Models*, Oxford University Press, New York, 1991), provide econometric evidence, using quarterly data for 1961–1987, that the Phillips Curve has existed as a stable relationship in the United States over that considerable period of time, including the 1970s.

cent in 30 years, few people would have been hurt. In fact, 5 percent is an average between the much higher annual rates that did hurt during the oil-price-shocked 1970s, and lower rates at other times. And it was the short-run acceleration, not the long-run compounding, that presented economic and political problems.

In 1959, Sumner Slichter, a relatively conservative business-oriented economist, wrote:

> . . . that inflation is not a temporary phenomenon, due to acute but passing maladjustments, but that it is a lasting phenomenon, due to built-in characteristics of the economy that are not easily changed. . . . The greatest harm and waste caused by inflation and fear of inflation is that they have made both government and industry afraid of expansionist policies and have deprived the country of billions of dollars of production and millions of manyears of employment which the country could have had if it had not made a fetish of a stable price level.[7]

True, 1959 was a long time ago: The strong labor unions that were then central to inflationary phenomena have largely disappeared, for example; and still to come were the the oil-price shocks of the 1970s, the huge deficits of the 1980s, and the health-cost crisis of the 1990s. In 1959, inflation of consumer prices had averaged 3 percent per year over the previous decade; in 1991, it had averaged 4 percent. Economist Larry Summers, before he became undersecretary of the treasury, suggested that 2–3 percent remains a proper target now.[8]

Whatever the precise numbers, however, the basic point remains: Some degree of inflation is a probable concomitant of growth. It is institutionally difficult and painful to instill downward price flexibility in modern economies, and a society in which a price and income must go down for every price and income that go up, is likely to be a sour and critical society. To be sure, this may be considered a psychological problem rather than an economic one: Economists use the term "monetary illusion" to point out that real incomes and other returns are what people live on, not inflated current-dollar ones.

---

[7]Sumner H. Slichter, "Inflation—A Problem of Shrinking Importance," in John T. Dunlop, ed., *Potentials of the American Economy: Selected Essays of Sumner H. Slichter*, Harvard University Press, Cambridge, Mass., 1961, pp. 135–149.

[8]Cited in *The Economist*, November 7–13, 1992, p. 23.

Nonetheless, the psychology does affect real economic decisions (e.g., investment) and real political and personal decisions, so the nominal rapidly becomes real.

Why might some economists and others adhere to a zero-inflation target? One reason is that the sheer deductive logic upon which most economic theory is based leads to the conclusion that the profit-maximization axiom of economics *must* lead to behavior based on rational expectations: Once it is clear that year-to-year inflation is the norm, maximizing behavior will anticipate future inflation, raising prices or wages in advance. That, in turn, will accelerate future inflation, leading to an actual-inflation–expected-inflation spiral that will inevitably accelerate out of hand; the only vaccine is zero inflation. The trouble with this argument, however, is that it is not borne out empirically; expectations and behavior in response to expectations are much more complex and variable than simple extrapolations of further inflation.

Another argument for zero inflation is that hyper-inflationary spirals do happen. They happened in Germany after both world wars and in Brazil in the 1970s and 1980s, and a similar phenomenon is apparently beginning in Russia in the 1990s. In fact, the lessons of these economies for the United States are very limited, if they exist at all, but they do condition the psychology of economists themselves.

More centrally, however, the roots of American fears of hyper-inflation and the consequent advocacy of zero-inflation targets may well be fertilized by some of this history of hyper-inflation elsewhere, but they are planted in the soil of the United States. In the 1970s, U.S. inflation accelerated to rates much higher than they had ever been in peacetime: The annual average increase in the consumer price index (CPI) from the first oil-shock stemming from the Yom Kippur War of 1973 through the end of the shocks in 1981 was 9.3 percent; the peak in 1980 was 13.5 percent. For an economy in which 3 percent had been considered a norm, this seemed to some people to presage a move toward hyper-inflation if discipline were lost.

The flaw in this fearful line of reasoning, however, was that discipline had little to do with it, and expectations probably not much more. Rather, the underlying cause was the initial oil shock of 1973 and the reverberations of that and the additional shocks through the rest of the decade. From 1973 to 1981, annual fuel-price increases averaged

20.8 percent; in the first of these years, the increase was 33.3 percent. The result was described by Robert Gordon in an analysis both of post–World War II economic history through 1979 and the contemporary reactions of economic theorists to that history:

> . . . a common feature of all adverse supply shocks is that the division of any given level of nominal GNP is shifted toward a higher price level and a lower level of GNP.   An expansive or "accommodating" demand policy can moderate the impact on real GNP only at the cost of raising the price level and aggravating inflation.   Restrictive or "extinguishing" demand policy can moderate the price increase only at the cost of further aggravating the shortfall of real GNP. . . .

> During the 1973–1979 decade, the analysis of supply shocks consumed relatively little space in academic journals as compared to the implications for economic policy of the "rational expectations hypothesis". . . . Although it caused much ferment in academic circles and many heated conference exchanges, the [rational expectations] theorem had little impact on policymakers, because its underlying supply hypothesis depended on instantaneous price flexibility and thus seemed more applicable to price-taking yeoman farmers than to the price-setting institutions of the post-war United States. . . .

> Different standards must be applied in judging policymakers who are forced to react to supply shocks and those who live in a relatively peaceful world in which demand stability is the only problem.[9]

In the United States, however, presidents Ford and Carter were both faced with "stagflation," trade-offs between high unemployment and low inflation that had no palatable answers: Any acceptable level of employment would induce unacceptable rates of inflation; any acceptable rate of inflation would induce unacceptable unemployment. Both Ford and Carter were defeated after their first terms in

---

[9]Robert J. Gordon, "Postwar Macroeconomics: The Evolution of Events and Ideas," in Martin J. Feldstein, ed., *The Economy in Transition*, University of Chicago Press, Chicago, Ill., 1980, pp. 146–153. Much study of rational expectations has taken place since 1980, and Gordon might now modify some of the judgments he made at that time.

office, but the oil-price-induced difficulties were not limited to the United States: Within two years of Carter's defeat, Callaghan in Britain, Schmidt in Germany, Giscard d'Estaing in France, and both Trudeau and Clark in Canada lost elections or were otherwise forced out of office. Most of them were liberals (in the American sense) losing to conservatives, but in France, Mitterand's replacement of Giscard was a move to the left; the only common thread seems to be their inability to solve political problems stemming from the sour oil-shock-induced worldwide economy of the 1970s.

What happened in the 1980s is less clear. Figure 4.1 shows unemployment and inflation in the United States, and their sum, sometimes termed the "Misery Index."[10]   The summary curve illustrates clearly the "stagflation" of the 1970s; additionally, the curve showing

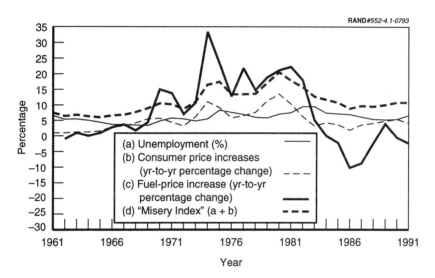

SOURCE: *Economic Report of the President, 1992*, Tables B-30 and B-56.

Figure 4.1—The "Misery Index" and Its Components

---

[10]The term was coined by the Reagan Administration, but in fact, unemployment—a year-by-year statistic—and inflation—a change *from* one year to the next—are in no sense additive.

fuel-price changes tends to bear out the relationship to the oil shocks. With the end of the shocks, unemployment and inflation returned to near the levels of the early 1970s, which were considered uncomfortable at the time but now look pretty good relative to the subsequent period. At the time, the 1980s seemed to feel good to the American people, as indicated by the Reagan landslide of 1984 and Bush's victory in 1988; the constancy of government in the other major industrial nations was the same.

Yet, the unacceptability of such unemployment levels, rising again because of recession and slow growth around the world, is becoming evident. Not only did Bush lose the 1992 election, but in 1993, prime ministers Mulroney of Canada and Miyazawa of Japan were ousted. Britain's John Major, who had been returned by a thin margin in 1992, was in deep trouble in his own party. Major, in a June 1993 interview, blamed the worldwide recession not only for his political troubles and those of President Clinton, but also for the difficulties encountered by Miyazawa, prime ministers Ciampi of Italy and Gonzalez of Spain, presidents Mitterand of France and Yeltsin of Russia, and Chancellor Kohl of Germany.[11]

Why this has become the case is not a major issue for this report. In the United States, it may be a combination of the discomfort with current 10–11 percent summary levels of inflation plus unemployment; a belief that the combination of the high budgetary and trade deficits resulting from Reagan policies, and the consequent high interest rates, means that things cannot get better for a long time; and the middle-class feelings discussed earlier about escalation of key costs, deterioration of public goods, and increasing maldistribution of income. For the world, the effect of the malaise in the U.S. economy, much the largest, is one central factor.

But Germany, the third-largest economy, has also contributed to world decline. The cost of reconstructing the East German economy after unification has raised problems similar to those of the oil shocks: With no palatable available combinations of unemployment–economic growth and price stability, the memory of historical German hyper-inflations (a memory that provides the German

---

[11]Thomas Plate and William Tuohy, "John Major: Even Under Fire, Britain's Prime Minister Holds His Own," *Los Angeles Times*, June 20, 1993, p. M3.

equivalent of Churchill's gold standard and the American deficit) has led the Bundesbank to opt for stability at all costs. The consequent stagnation and unemployment have spread throughout Europe. The cost of reconstructing the rest of the former communist lands, including Russia, has had similar effects, although lesser ones because they can be ignored by the wealthy nations for the short run. And Japan's different economic problems are spreading in different ways.

It is not clear how well the United States can insulate itself from the other negative factors in the world economy—or whether it should try. Politically, it seems likely that the attempt to accelerate the growth of U.S. economy will be made. American acceleration without American insulation is likely, in turn, to be the best tonic for the world economy. Yet, if German policies continue to repress European growth, and if Japan tries to revive its own economy by increasing its trade surplus, then the U.S. will almost inevitably attempt to combine accelerated domestic growth with external protection. That combination will not be good for the world nor, in the long run, for the United States, but it is not the central subject of this report.

Rather, the primary point of this chapter is that the high-employment and stable-price objectives for the United States economy may trade against one another, at least for the short run. The trade-off may be an impossible one as in the 1970s, or it may be easier as it seems to be now. It is constrained by the United States' increasingly close relationship with the world economy, but the U.S. economy is still large enough to contemplate insulation and/or protection if that seems called for by politics or economics. And all these trade-offs play against—or reinforce—the other major American economic objectives.

Chapter Five

CONCLUSIONS FOR U.S. ECONOMIC STRATEGY: NEGATIVE AND POSITIVE

The major conclusion for U.S. economic strategy is the negative one:

> *Reduction of the budget deficit should not be the single central ob-jective of long-run macroeconomic strategy. Deficit reduction is instrumental to certain other important objectives: stabilizing for-eign ownership of American assets, removing inhibitions to an active fiscal policy and to spending for public needs, and keeping interest payments on the national debt from becoming the 1990s-and-beyond burden that health care has been for the last decade. But the role of the deficit in regard to other needs, particularly growth in standards of living, is ambiguous at best. Too strong an emphasis on the deficit can potentially depress and distress the U.S. economy over a very long run.*

This conclusion has a variety of implications for current economic policy:

- This report has provided little discussion of long run versus short run as a current issue, or of the need for current stimulus. Nonetheless, the implication of downgrading what has been stated as the central long-run consideration, deficit reduction, could imply at least by default a greater emphasis on short-run considerations than would otherwise be the case.

- The examination of the trade-offs between high employment and price stability has also suggested placing a greater weight on economic stimulus to increase employment than on prices as such. Specific current policy must be evaluated on the basis of specific current data, however, and on projections, including projected expectations, based on those data.

- Abstracting from distributional concerns, increasing standards of living remain the major objective of economic policy, and increasing standards remain dependent primarily on increasing productivity. Since increasing productivity seems to depend more on technological advance than on increased investment as such, public resources used to promote increased productivity—to the extent feasible—via direct or tax expenditures, should focus more on promotion and adoption of technology than on incentives to investment as such. Education and training of the labor force should also be an important competitor in this game.

- Encouraging private investment, and also private expenditures on technology (e.g., research and development), may depend more on increased consumer demand than on increased personal savings. The savings issue, too, must be examined in terms of specific data for a specific time.

- Prime consideration should be given to the competition for resources of public investment versus private investment in encouraging productivity. The marginal public dollar, or billion dollars, may provide a higher productivity return if spent on education, training, or transportation than it would on encouraging private investment in more commercial office space. But this does not mean that a billion dollars should be diverted from private investment in new-process steel mills in order to finance entitlement programs for rich farmers. The answer for each case depends on the specifics of that case.

- Public investment versus private investment is an economic question, at least conceptually. Filling of public needs, other than for investment (to the extent the distinction can be made) versus filling of private needs—e.g., the value of a park or police protection versus the value of an addition to private after-tax income—must be resolved politically, but that does not make it an unimportant or meaningless issue.

- Withal, for reasons discussed, the deficit cannot be ignored. Paying attention to it does not mean that it must be rapidly brought down to zero, however. One measure of the burden of the national debt, to which the deficit adds each year, is the interest that must be paid on the debt. That interest, in turn, depends on the size of the debt, not the size of the deficit as such. To provide an example of an alternative rule for controlling the deficit, suppose, then, that, instead of a zero-deficit goal, the policy was promulgated so that the deficit must not increase the debt as a proportion of GDP (or, in order to keep from exaggerating the business cycle, a proportion of potential GDP at some stated level of employment). In 1991, the interest-bearing national debt was $3.7 trillion, about 65 percent of the GDP. If GDP were to increase at a normal 3.5 percent per year, comparable with that of the 1960s, that would mean an annual deficit no greater than about $130 billion, much less than it is now, but a more plausible goal than zero to be achieved and then maintained. In any case, the easiest way to reduce the deficit is by economic growth producing increased tax revenues. Timing of reduction should be closely related to timing of growth.

The deficit is certainly not irrelevant to the national well-being of the United States. The gold standard was not irrelevant to the national well-being of the United Kingdom in the 1920s. But substituting deficit reduction for real national economic objectives—regularly improving standards of living, filling public as well as private needs, maintaining high employment and price stability, taking control over our country's own economic destiny, and appropriately distributing economic rewards—would be a grave error now as it was in the 1920s of Keynes and Churchill.

NATIONAL NEEDS

Table A.1 repeats text Table 3.1, showing broad categories of national needs, as estimated by their advocates or, in cases where advocates might want to minimize costs, by skeptics interested in estimating full costs. The remainder of this Appendix provides more detailed estimates within the categories, and their sources. "Minor" increases, below $5 billion or so, are not included except when the needs in question have recently been discussed in terms that may lead to perceptions that their costs would be higher than seems likely.

GENERAL URBAN: $20 BILLION

General urban needs are summarized in Table A.2 and itemized in the following subsections.

Housing: $15 Billion

"It would take $20 billion to clean up America's public housing and make it ready to sell. It would take another $10 billion per year to get every poverty-level household on to housing assistance—in effect a tax credit for the poor" (*The Economist*, April 11–17, 1992, p. 27). It is not completely clear that this is meant as an addition to the $15 billion currently being spent for housing for the lowest-income quintile of population, but in context it probably is. Although, if *The Economist*'s proposals to subsidize the sale of public housing to its

Table A.1

Annual Federal Full-Funding for Public Needs: The Advocates' View

Need	Funding ($ billions)
Housing and other urban needs. Education, training, and other needs within cities are counted separately.	20
Education, from preschool through higher education. The largest component is for a full preschool program; additional federal aid for kindergarten through high school is the smallest.	50
Training, mostly for a new "apprenticeship" program.	16
Public assistance. The bulk of this would go not for income support as such but for "workfare" and other public jobs.	40
Physical infrastructure. The largest component is for highways, but the total is spread over urban transit, water supply, sewers, etc.	40
International, mostly economic, development assistance to the "third world," at the scope requested by the nations in this category at the Rio environmental conference. Aid to Eastern Europe is substantially less.	50
Space, mostly to put a man on Mars.	11
TOTAL	227

Table A.2

General Urban Needs

Need	Funding ($ billions)
Housing	15
Other	5

occupants worked, the ultimate costs might be less than at present; most costs should be counted as initially incremental. This calculation amortizes the $20 billion fix-up cost over four years.

Other: $5 Billion

The Eisenhower Foundation is quoted as estimating that "basic inner city social and education programs" would cost $30 billion per year (*The Economist*, May 22–29, 1992, p. 26); the U.S. Conference of Mayors asks $34 billion (*The Economist*, May 9–15, 1992). The bulk of such figures is included in other categories here, however—e.g., housing, education, and training. Nonetheless, a significant category of expenditures covers urban improvement that is neither housing nor training, education, etc. In recent years, the federal budget has included $3.5–$4 billion for "Urban Renewal and Community Development"; at the beginning of the 1980s, the figure was above $5 billion in current dollars. New proposals such as "Enterprise Zones" might in themselves run $1 billion or so per year. The $5-billion estimate here is arbitrary but not likely to be far off for full funding of the "needs" seen by the advocates of radically improving America's cities.

EDUCATION AND RELATED: $50 BILLION

Education and related needs are summarized in Table A.3 and are itemized in the following subsections.

Table A.3

Educational Needs

Need	Funding ($ billions)
Preschool +	20
Kindergarten–12th grade	6–10
Higher education	15

Preschool + : $20 Billion

President Bush's "1993 budget requested . . . annual Head Start spending [of] $2.8 billion. But boosters of the federal preschool program argue that $6.9 billion is needed to fully finance Head Start" (*National Journal*, April 11, 1992, p. 873). The $6.9 billion would extend current Head Start programs to every eligible poor child. But Julius Richmond, the father of Head Start, and Lisbeth Schorr, the mother of the 1960s program of health centers for the poor, argue that the United States should use "the structure of Head Start, which helps just 4-year olds, to finance and organize an array of services and family supports that begin before birth," and continue at least until the child enters school (*Los Angeles Times*, June 23, 1992, p. B-7). Their estimate is that this would cost an additional $20 billion per year. The sum includes major increases in nutritional and health spending for the poor that would otherwise be carried in a separate budget category, which is why this segment is called here "Preschool+."

Kindergarten–12th Grade: $6–$10 Billion

The proposals here are so multifold, and the question of the division among federal, state, and local funding so unresolved, that no single estimate of incremental federal costs is available. The $6–$10 billion is a current best guess of RAND experts (some of whom are currently working on a more refined set of estimates) for a needs-covering increase in the current $6 billion federal contribution to programs for compensatory aid to disadvantaged students. The $6–$10 billion envelope can also be presumed to cover any restructuring, such as that proposed by the Bush Administration to substitute a program of school vouchers for direct aid to the public schools.

Higher Education: $15 Billion

In addition to the panoply of research grants going to universities, no significant increase in which has been proposed, current federal assistance to higher education is extended primarily through a set of "Pell grants" (after the Senator from Rhode Island) to lower-income students, and through guaranteed student loans to those who are better off. The annual cost is $10 billion. The House Subcommittee on Post-Secondary Education has proposed expanding the grant program to include higher-income students and changing it to an "entitlement program," which makes support available to everyone fitting the eligibility criteria, rather than extending funding out of a closed-end appropriation on a case-by-case basis. The estimated total cost is $20 billion per year (*Congressional Quarterly*, October 12, 1991, p. 2959), which, considering the fact that grants would be substituted for repayable loans, is estimated here at an incremental level of $15 billion.

TRAINING: $16 BILLION

Training needs are summarized in Table A.4 and are itemized in the following subsections.

Vocational Training: $6 Billion

Economist Sar Levitan, who has been following training needs for several decades, estimates that full funding of current federal vocational training programs would take $16.5 billion per year, as compared with the current $10.1 billion (*Los Angeles Times*, June 2, 1992, p. A-3; and private conversation).

Apprenticeship: $15 Billion

Considerable attention has been paid recently to the need for an American program, similar to those in Germany and elsewhere, providing skills training through an apprenticeship system for those youth not going to college. According to *The National Journal*

Table A.4

Training Needs

Need	Funding ($ billions)
Vocational training	6
Apprenticeship	10

May 2, 1992), "to secure an ongoing financial underpinning for apprenticeship training, the Commission on the Skills of the American Workforce had recommended a play-or-pay scheme under which businesses could either spend 1 percent of their payroll on training their frontline workers or put 1 percent of their payroll into a national kitty to do that." The 1 percent would be more than $30 billion. But, considering the amount of training that businesses do already, a $10-billion increment might be a better estimate.

PUBLIC ASSISTANCE AND RELATED: $43 BILLION

Social analyst Mickey Kaus estimates that the incremental annual cost of a revised public-assistance program that would provide public jobs for all those who could work and could not find private jobs, and income support above the poverty line for those who could not work, would be $43–$59 billion (*The End of Equality*, Basic Books, New York, 1992). The proposal is similar to one first put forward by the Office of Economic Opportunity in 1965, and the costs are consistent, given inflation. The estimate is for federal, state, and local costs, but, pragmatically, the increment would have to be almost entirely federal. Because of potential overlap with both the urban and the training proposals discussed above, however, the estimate here is at the bottom of Kaus' range, and even it may be a bit high.

INFRASTRUCTURE AND ENVIRONMENT: $40 BILLION

This very large category is not estimated piece by piece as was done with the others (see Table A.5). Infrastructure is a very complex and esoteric category, with overlapping components and a complicated funding structure made up of federal contributions, many of which are gathered into and spent out of trust funds, and state and local expenditures, which in some categories are larger than federal and in some categories, smaller. These estimates are based primarily on the Congressional Budget Office (CBO) study, *New Directions for the Nation's Public Works*, September 1988. The CBO document (p. 129) cites the National Council on Public Works Improvement as concluding "that national infrastructure outlays should be increased by as much as 100 percent," i.e., doubling current expenditures.

Table A.5

Infrastructure and Environmental Needs

Need	Funding ($ billions)
Highways	15
Mass transit	5
Aviation	7
Water transportation	2
Wastewater treatment	4
Solid waste	5

(CBO thinks this is substantially too high, but the object of the current analysis is to compile the estimates of *advocates* of expenditures for full-funding for national needs.)

Table A.5, then, applies the doubling rule to a summary table on page 12 of the CBO publication, which estimates federal infrastructure spending by category in 1988. In addition to doubling (making the increments equal to the base numbers in the original table), estimates are adjusted upward because of inflation since 1988, and because the current condition of state and local finances implies that the federal government would have to contribute more than its 1988 share of the total increment.

The CBO table lists as one category "Wastewater treatment." Elsewhere, however, the Environmental Protection Agency is quoted as estimating "that cities will have to spend at least $54 billion by the year 2000 to meet just a portion of new and proposed regulations for solid waste and clean water" (*Washington Post*, April 18, 1992, p. D10). Making what seems the safe assumption—that if these increments are spent, they will ultimately be supported by the federal government—an additional line is added to Table A.5 for an estimate of the "Solid waste" portion, not already included in the "Wastewater" line from the CBO table.

INTERNATIONAL: $40–$50 BILLION

International needs are summarized in Table A.6 and are itemized in the following subsections.

Table A.6

International Needs

Need	Funding ($ billions)
Peacekeeping	1
Rehabilitation of reactors	1
Aid to CIS	3–12
Aid to other former Eastern Bloc	3–5
Development aid	30

Peacekeeping: $1 Billion

The Economist, May 23–29, 1992, p. 44, reports that the UN "peacekeeping bill for the next 12 months is put at $2.7 billion." The U.S. share might be of the order of $1 billion.

Rehabilitation of Reactors: $1 Billion

The *National Journal*, May 16, 1992, p. 1206, quotes Ivan Selin, Chairman of the Nuclear Regulatory Commission, to the effect that the cost of bringing Soviet-built nuclear reactors up to standard would exceed $10 billion. Spreading that cost over five years and assuming the U.S. share to be about half makes the annual cost about $1 billion, not all of which would be incremental.

Aid to CIS: $3–$12 Billion

The cost of the "Grand Bargain" proposed before the breakup of the Soviet Union by Soviet economist Grigor Yavlinsky and a number of Harvard dons was about $3 billion annually to the U.S. Although the *annual* U.S. contribution to the West's proposed stabilization package of $24 billion (over more than one year) to the former Soviet Union is difficult to estimate, it seems consistent with that figure. But in terms of full funding of needs, *The Economist*, July 4–10, 1992, p. 20, quotes David Roche of Morgan Stanley as estimating $76–$167 billion over five years needed for everything except environmental cleanup and ruble-stabilization, $15–$33 billion per year, up to perhaps $12 billion for the U.S. share.

Aid to Other Former Eastern Bloc: $3–$5 Billion

This is simply set at the lower end of estimated aid to the former Soviet Union.

Development Aid: $30 Billion

The Rio de Janeiro conference on the environment set 0.7 percent of GNP as a goal for development aid from the rich nations. For the United States, this would come to about $40 billion, or an increment of about $30 billion over the $11 billion it spends today.

To calibrate the $40–$50 billion international category, almost all of which consists of assistance to other countries, the United States' contribution to the Marshall Plan over a five-year period was about 2 percent of GNP, which today would be in excess of $100 billion.

SPACE: $11 BILLION ($4–$18 BILLION)

Space needs are summarized in Table A.7 and are itemized in the following subsections.

Space Station: $3 Billion

"NASA projects [it] will cost $30 billion before it [space station] can be occupied permanently in 1999" (*Aviation Week and Space Technology*, July 1, 1991, p. 20). Thirty billion dollars over the nine years from 1991 to 1999 is about $3 billion per year.

Table A.7

Space Needs

Need	Funding ($ billions)
Space station	3
Man on Mars	1–15

Man on Mars: $1–$15 Billion

This is a very wide spread. The operative quotation, from another article in *Aviation Week and Space Technology* (also July 1, 1991, p. 20), is

> A joint U.S./Soviet/European/Japanese manned Mars effort could put explorers on the planet within 21 years at one-third the cost of U.S. options, if the project focused on use of Soviet Energia heavy-lift boosters, according to a study by Stanford University and Soviet engineers. The international effort, using existing technologies, could launch and assemble the initial stage of a Mars base for about $60 billion over 20 years, compared with estimates up to $540 billion for NASA options, the group found.

Sixty billion dollars with the costs divided three or four ways over 20 years is $1 billion. Five hundred and forty billion dollars over 20 years is $27 billion per year. But since the United States has already begun to talk about sharing this heavy cost with other national partners, the assumption here is that the federal budget would carry little more than half, or about $15 billion.

In order to simplify an estimate that is at best an order of magnitude in any case, the $4–$18 billion estimate for space is split halfway at $11 billion in Table A.1.